50 Dutch Oven Dessert Making Recipes for Home

By: Kelly Johnson

Table of Contents

- Dutch Oven Peach Cobbler
- Dutch Oven Apple Crisp
- Dutch Oven Cherry Clafoutis
- Dutch Oven Pineapple Upside-Down Cake
- Dutch Oven Chocolate Lava Cake
- Dutch Oven Blueberry Bread Pudding
- Dutch Oven Lemon Bars
- Dutch Oven Banana Bread
- Dutch Oven Strawberry Shortcake
- Dutch Oven Mixed Berry Crumble
- Dutch Oven Pumpkin Pie
- Dutch Oven Cinnamon Rolls
- Dutch Oven S'mores Dip
- Dutch Oven Pear Tart
- Dutch Oven Raspberry Swirl Cheesecake
- Dutch Oven Apricot Cobbler
- Dutch Oven Fig and Walnut Cake
- Dutch Oven Blackberry Cobbler
- Dutch Oven Plum Clafoutis
- Dutch Oven Orange Pound Cake
- Dutch Oven Pecan Pie
- Dutch Oven Cranberry Crisp
- Dutch Oven Rhubarb Crumble
- Dutch Oven Coconut Macaroons
- Dutch Oven Espresso Brownies
- Dutch Oven Almond Cake
- Dutch Oven Gingerbread
- Dutch Oven Date Bars
- Dutch Oven Cherry Chocolate Chip Cookies
- Dutch Oven Butterscotch Blondies
- Dutch Oven Hazelnut Torte
- Dutch Oven Lemon Poppy Seed Cake
- Dutch Oven Oatmeal Raisin Cookies
- Dutch Oven Peach Melba
- Dutch Oven Pistachio Cake

- Dutch Oven Raspberry Chocolate Tart
- Dutch Oven Snickerdoodle Bars
- Dutch Oven Tiramisu
- Dutch Oven Upside-Down Pear Cake
- Dutch Oven Walnut Brownies
- Dutch Oven Zucchini Bread
- Dutch Oven Cranberry Orange Cake
- Dutch Oven Maple Pecan Pie
- Dutch Oven Apple Cranberry Crisp
- Dutch Oven Chocolate Chip Cookie Bars
- Dutch Oven Lemon Meringue Pie
- Dutch Oven Red Velvet Cake
- Dutch Oven Carrot Cake
- Dutch Oven Mint Chocolate Chip Brownies
- Dutch Oven Coconut Cream Pie

Dutch Oven Peach Cobbler

Ingredients:

- 6 cups sliced peaches (fresh or canned)
- 1 cup granulated sugar
- 1/4 teaspoon ground cinnamon
- 1/4 teaspoon ground nutmeg
- 1 tablespoon lemon juice
- 1 cup all-purpose flour
- 1 cup granulated sugar
- 1 teaspoon baking powder
- 1/4 teaspoon salt
- 1/2 cup unsalted butter, melted
- 1/2 cup milk
- 1 teaspoon vanilla extract

Instructions:

1. Preheat your Dutch oven by placing coals beneath and on top of it. If you're using an oven, preheat it to 350°F (175°C).
2. In a large bowl, combine the sliced peaches, 1 cup sugar, cinnamon, nutmeg, and lemon juice. Stir well to coat the peaches evenly. Let the mixture sit for about 10-15 minutes to allow the flavors to meld.
3. In another bowl, mix together the flour, 1 cup sugar, baking powder, and salt.
4. Stir in the melted butter, milk, and vanilla extract until just combined. The batter will be thick.
5. Pour the peach mixture into the preheated Dutch oven.
6. Spoon the batter over the peaches, spreading it out as evenly as possible.
7. Cover the Dutch oven with its lid and place it over the preheated coals. If using an oven, place the Dutch oven on a baking sheet and bake for about 40-45 minutes, or until the top is golden brown and the filling is bubbly.
8. Serve the peach cobbler warm, optionally with a scoop of vanilla ice cream on top. Enjoy!

Dutch Oven Apple Crisp

Ingredients:

For the Apple Filling:

- 6 cups of thinly sliced apples (peeled and cored)
- 1/4 cup granulated sugar
- 2 tablespoons all-purpose flour
- 1 teaspoon ground cinnamon
- 1/4 teaspoon ground nutmeg
- 1 tablespoon lemon juice

For the Crisp Topping:

- 1 cup old-fashioned oats
- 1/2 cup all-purpose flour
- 1/2 cup packed brown sugar
- 1/4 teaspoon ground cinnamon
- 1/2 cup unsalted butter, softened

Instructions:

1. Preheat your Dutch oven by placing coals beneath and on top of it. If you're using an oven, preheat it to 350°F (175°C).
2. In a large bowl, combine the sliced apples, granulated sugar, flour, cinnamon, nutmeg, and lemon juice. Stir well to coat the apples evenly.
3. In another bowl, mix together the oats, flour, brown sugar, and cinnamon for the crisp topping.
4. Cut the softened butter into small pieces and add it to the oat mixture. Use your hands or a fork to mix until the mixture resembles coarse crumbs.
5. Spread the apple mixture evenly in the bottom of the preheated Dutch oven.
6. Sprinkle the crisp topping over the apples, covering them completely.
7. Cover the Dutch oven with its lid and place it over the preheated coals. If using an oven, place the Dutch oven on a baking sheet and bake for about 40-45 minutes, or until the topping is golden brown and the apples are tender.

8. Let the apple crisp cool for a few minutes before serving. Enjoy it warm, optionally with a scoop of vanilla ice cream or a dollop of whipped cream on top.

Dutch Oven Cherry Clafoutis

Ingredients:

- 2 cups fresh cherries, pitted
- 3 large eggs
- 1/2 cup granulated sugar
- 1 cup whole milk
- 1/2 cup all-purpose flour
- 1 teaspoon vanilla extract
- Pinch of salt
- Powdered sugar, for dusting (optional)

Instructions:

1. Preheat your Dutch oven by placing coals beneath and on top of it. If you're using an oven, preheat it to 350°F (175°C).
2. Grease the bottom and sides of the Dutch oven with butter or cooking spray.
3. Arrange the pitted cherries in a single layer on the bottom of the Dutch oven.
4. In a mixing bowl, whisk together the eggs and granulated sugar until well combined.
5. Add the milk, flour, vanilla extract, and a pinch of salt to the egg mixture. Whisk until smooth and no lumps remain.
6. Pour the batter over the cherries in the Dutch oven, ensuring they are evenly covered.
7. Cover the Dutch oven with its lid and place it over the preheated coals. If using an oven, place the Dutch oven on a baking sheet and bake for about 30-35 minutes, or until the clafoutis is set and lightly golden on top.
8. Remove the Dutch oven from the heat or oven and let the clafoutis cool for a few minutes.
9. Dust the top of the clafoutis with powdered sugar, if desired, before serving. Enjoy this classic French dessert warm or at room temperature.

Dutch Oven Pineapple Upside-Down Cake

Ingredients:

For the topping:

- 1/4 cup unsalted butter
- 3/4 cup packed brown sugar
- 1 can (20 oz) pineapple slices, drained
- Maraschino cherries (optional)

For the cake batter:

- 1 1/2 cups all-purpose flour
- 1 1/2 teaspoons baking powder
- 1/2 teaspoon salt
- 1/2 cup unsalted butter, softened
- 1 cup granulated sugar
- 2 large eggs
- 1 teaspoon vanilla extract
- 1/2 cup pineapple juice (reserved from the canned pineapple)
- 1/4 cup milk

Instructions:

1. Preheat your Dutch oven by placing coals beneath and on top of it. If you're using an oven, preheat it to 350°F (175°C).
2. In the Dutch oven, melt 1/4 cup of butter over the preheated coals or on the stovetop.
3. Sprinkle the brown sugar evenly over the melted butter in the Dutch oven.
4. Arrange the pineapple slices on top of the brown sugar, placing them close together to cover the bottom of the Dutch oven. You can place maraschino cherries in the center of each pineapple slice if desired.
5. In a mixing bowl, whisk together the flour, baking powder, and salt.
6. In another mixing bowl, cream together the softened butter and granulated sugar until light and fluffy.

7. Beat in the eggs, one at a time, followed by the vanilla extract.
8. Gradually add the dry ingredients to the wet ingredients, alternating with the pineapple juice and milk, until everything is well combined and you have a smooth batter.
9. Carefully pour the cake batter over the pineapple slices in the Dutch oven, spreading it out evenly.
10. Cover the Dutch oven with its lid and place it over the preheated coals. If using an oven, place the Dutch oven on a baking sheet and bake for about 30-35 minutes, or until a toothpick inserted into the center of the cake comes out clean.
11. Once the cake is done, remove it from the heat and let it cool in the Dutch oven for a few minutes.
12. To serve, carefully invert the Dutch oven onto a serving platter, allowing the pineapple upside-down cake to release onto the platter. Serve warm and enjoy!

Dutch Oven Chocolate Lava Cake

Ingredients:

- 1/2 cup (1 stick) unsalted butter
- 4 ounces semi-sweet chocolate, chopped
- 2 large eggs
- 2 large egg yolks
- 1/4 cup granulated sugar
- 1 teaspoon vanilla extract
- 2 tablespoons all-purpose flour
- Pinch of salt
- Cooking spray or butter, for greasing

Instructions:

1. Preheat your Dutch oven by placing coals beneath and on top of it. If you're using an oven, preheat it to 375°F (190°C).
2. In a microwave-safe bowl or saucepan, melt the butter and chopped chocolate together, stirring occasionally until smooth. Set aside to cool slightly.
3. In a separate mixing bowl, whisk together the eggs, egg yolks, granulated sugar, and vanilla extract until well combined.
4. Gradually pour the melted chocolate mixture into the egg mixture, stirring continuously until smooth.
5. Sift the flour and salt into the chocolate mixture and fold gently until just combined. Be careful not to overmix.
6. Grease the bottom and sides of your Dutch oven with cooking spray or butter.
7. Pour the chocolate batter into the greased Dutch oven, spreading it out evenly.
8. Cover the Dutch oven with its lid and place it over the preheated coals. If using an oven, place the Dutch oven on a baking sheet and bake for about 12-15 minutes, or until the edges are set but the center is still slightly jiggly.
9. Once done, remove the Dutch oven from the heat and let it sit for a couple of minutes to cool slightly.
10. Carefully spoon the chocolate lava cake onto serving plates and serve immediately. Optionally, you can dust with powdered sugar or serve with a scoop of vanilla ice cream or whipped cream. Enjoy the rich and decadent chocolate lava cake!

Dutch Oven Blueberry Bread Pudding

Ingredients:

- 6 cups cubed day-old bread (such as French bread or brioche)
- 1 1/2 cups fresh blueberries (or frozen, thawed)
- 4 large eggs
- 2 cups milk
- 1/2 cup granulated sugar
- 1 teaspoon vanilla extract
- 1/2 teaspoon ground cinnamon
- Pinch of salt
- Butter, for greasing the Dutch oven

For the sauce (optional):

- 1/2 cup unsalted butter
- 1 cup granulated sugar
- 1/2 cup heavy cream
- 1 teaspoon vanilla extract

Instructions:

1. Preheat your Dutch oven by placing coals beneath and on top of it. If you're using an oven, preheat it to 350°F (175°C).
2. Grease the bottom and sides of the Dutch oven with butter.
3. In a large mixing bowl, combine the cubed bread and blueberries. Toss gently to distribute the blueberries evenly throughout the bread.
4. In another mixing bowl, whisk together the eggs, milk, granulated sugar, vanilla extract, cinnamon, and salt until well combined.
5. Pour the egg mixture over the bread and blueberries, making sure all the bread is soaked in the liquid.
6. Transfer the bread pudding mixture to the greased Dutch oven, spreading it out evenly.

7. Cover the Dutch oven with its lid and place it over the preheated coals. If using an oven, place the Dutch oven on a baking sheet and bake for about 45-50 minutes, or until the bread pudding is set and golden brown on top.
8. While the bread pudding is baking, you can prepare the sauce (if using): In a small saucepan, melt the butter over medium heat. Stir in the sugar and heavy cream, and cook until the sugar is dissolved and the sauce is smooth. Remove from heat and stir in the vanilla extract.
9. Once the bread pudding is done, remove it from the heat and let it cool for a few minutes.
10. Serve the bread pudding warm, optionally drizzled with the prepared sauce. Enjoy this comforting and delicious dessert!

Dutch Oven Lemon Bars

Ingredients:

For the crust:

- 1 1/2 cups all-purpose flour
- 1/2 cup powdered sugar
- 3/4 cup unsalted butter, softened

For the lemon filling:

- 1 1/2 cups granulated sugar
- 1/4 cup all-purpose flour
- 4 large eggs
- 2/3 cup fresh lemon juice
- Zest of 2 lemons
- Powdered sugar, for dusting

Instructions:

1. Preheat your Dutch oven by placing coals beneath and on top of it. If you're using an oven, preheat it to 350°F (175°C).
2. In a mixing bowl, combine the flour, powdered sugar, and softened butter for the crust. Mix until crumbly and well combined.
3. Press the crust mixture evenly into the bottom of the greased Dutch oven.
4. Bake the crust in the preheated Dutch oven for about 20 minutes, or until lightly golden brown.
5. While the crust is baking, prepare the lemon filling. In a separate mixing bowl, whisk together the granulated sugar and flour.
6. Add the eggs, lemon juice, and lemon zest to the sugar mixture. Whisk until smooth and well combined.
7. Once the crust is baked, remove it from the Dutch oven and pour the lemon filling over the hot crust.
8. Return the Dutch oven to the heat or oven and bake for an additional 20-25 minutes, or until the filling is set and the edges are lightly golden.

9. Remove the Dutch oven from the heat or oven and let the lemon bars cool completely.
10. Once cooled, dust the top of the lemon bars with powdered sugar.
11. Slice the lemon bars into squares or rectangles and serve. Enjoy the tangy and sweet flavor of these Dutch Oven Lemon Bars!

Dutch Oven Banana Bread

Ingredients:

- 2 cups all-purpose flour
- 1 teaspoon baking soda
- 1/4 teaspoon salt
- 1/2 cup unsalted butter, softened
- 3/4 cup granulated sugar
- 2 large eggs
- 3 ripe bananas, mashed
- 1/4 cup milk
- 1 teaspoon vanilla extract
- Optional: chopped nuts, chocolate chips, or dried fruit for extra flavor (about 1/2 cup)

Instructions:

1. Preheat your Dutch oven by placing coals beneath and on top of it. If you're using an oven, preheat it to 350°F (175°C).
2. Grease the bottom and sides of your Dutch oven with butter or cooking spray.
3. In a mixing bowl, sift together the flour, baking soda, and salt. Set aside.
4. In another mixing bowl, cream together the softened butter and granulated sugar until light and fluffy.
5. Add the eggs to the butter-sugar mixture one at a time, beating well after each addition.
6. Stir in the mashed bananas, milk, and vanilla extract until well combined.
7. Gradually add the dry ingredients to the wet ingredients, mixing until just combined. Be careful not to overmix.
8. If desired, fold in any optional add-ins like chopped nuts, chocolate chips, or dried fruit.
9. Pour the batter into the greased Dutch oven, spreading it out evenly.
10. Cover the Dutch oven with its lid and place it over the preheated coals. If using an oven, place the Dutch oven on a baking sheet and bake for about 50-60 minutes, or until a toothpick inserted into the center comes out clean.
11. Once done, remove the Dutch oven from the heat or oven and let the banana bread cool for a few minutes.

12. Slice and serve the banana bread warm. Enjoy the moist and flavorful Dutch Oven Banana Bread as a delicious snack or breakfast treat!

Dutch Oven Strawberry Shortcake

Ingredients:

For the shortcakes:

- 2 cups all-purpose flour
- 1/4 cup granulated sugar
- 1 tablespoon baking powder
- 1/2 teaspoon salt
- 1/2 cup unsalted butter, cold and cut into small pieces
- 2/3 cup milk
- 1 teaspoon vanilla extract

For the strawberries:

- 4 cups fresh strawberries, hulled and sliced
- 1/4 cup granulated sugar

For the whipped cream:

- 1 cup heavy cream
- 2 tablespoons powdered sugar
- 1 teaspoon vanilla extract

Instructions:

1. Preheat your Dutch oven by placing coals beneath and on top of it. If you're using an oven, preheat it to 425°F (220°C).
2. In a large mixing bowl, whisk together the flour, sugar, baking powder, and salt.
3. Cut in the cold butter using a pastry cutter or your fingers until the mixture resembles coarse crumbs.
4. In a separate bowl, mix together the milk and vanilla extract.

5. Gradually pour the milk mixture into the dry ingredients, stirring until a soft dough forms.
6. Turn the dough out onto a floured surface and gently knead it a few times until it comes together.
7. Roll out the dough to about 1/2-inch thickness and use a biscuit cutter to cut out rounds of dough.
8. Place the rounds of dough onto the greased Dutch oven, leaving a little space between each one.
9. Cover the Dutch oven with its lid and place it over the preheated coals. If using an oven, place the Dutch oven on a baking sheet and bake for about 12-15 minutes, or until the shortcakes are golden brown and cooked through.
10. While the shortcakes are baking, prepare the strawberries by tossing them with the granulated sugar in a bowl. Let them sit for a few minutes to macerate and release their juices.
11. In another mixing bowl, whip the heavy cream, powdered sugar, and vanilla extract until stiff peaks form.
12. Once the shortcakes are done, remove them from the Dutch oven and let them cool slightly.
13. To assemble the strawberry shortcakes, split the shortcakes in half horizontally. Place a spoonful of strawberries on the bottom half of each shortcake, followed by a dollop of whipped cream. Top with the other half of the shortcake.
14. Serve the Dutch Oven Strawberry Shortcakes immediately and enjoy the delicious combination of tender shortcakes, sweet strawberries, and fluffy whipped cream!

Dutch Oven Mixed Berry Crumble

Ingredients:

For the berry filling:

- 4 cups mixed berries (such as strawberries, blueberries, raspberries, and blackberries)
- 1/4 cup granulated sugar
- 2 tablespoons cornstarch
- 1 tablespoon lemon juice
- Zest of 1 lemon

For the crumble topping:

- 1 cup old-fashioned oats
- 1/2 cup all-purpose flour
- 1/2 cup packed brown sugar
- 1/2 teaspoon ground cinnamon
- Pinch of salt
- 1/2 cup unsalted butter, melted

Instructions:

1. Preheat your Dutch oven by placing coals beneath and on top of it. If you're using an oven, preheat it to 375°F (190°C).
2. In a large mixing bowl, combine the mixed berries, granulated sugar, cornstarch, lemon juice, and lemon zest. Toss gently to coat the berries evenly.
3. In another mixing bowl, combine the oats, flour, brown sugar, cinnamon, and salt for the crumble topping.
4. Pour the melted butter over the dry ingredients for the crumble topping. Stir until the mixture resembles coarse crumbs.
5. Spread the berry mixture evenly in the bottom of the greased Dutch oven.
6. Sprinkle the crumble topping over the berries, covering them completely.

7. Cover the Dutch oven with its lid and place it over the preheated coals. If using an oven, place the Dutch oven on a baking sheet and bake for about 30-35 minutes, or until the topping is golden brown and the filling is bubbly.
8. Once done, remove the Dutch oven from the heat or oven and let the mixed berry crumble cool for a few minutes.
9. Serve the crumble warm, optionally with a scoop of vanilla ice cream or a dollop of whipped cream on top. Enjoy the sweet and tangy flavors of this Dutch Oven Mixed Berry Crumble!

Dutch Oven Pumpkin Pie

Ingredients:

For the crust:

- 1 1/4 cups all-purpose flour
- 1/2 teaspoon salt
- 1/2 teaspoon granulated sugar
- 1/2 cup unsalted butter, cold and cut into small cubes
- 2-4 tablespoons ice water

For the filling:

- 1 can (15 ounces) pumpkin puree
- 1 can (14 ounces) sweetened condensed milk
- 2 large eggs
- 1 teaspoon ground cinnamon
- 1/2 teaspoon ground ginger
- 1/4 teaspoon ground nutmeg
- 1/4 teaspoon ground cloves
- 1/2 teaspoon salt

Instructions:

1. Preheat your Dutch oven by placing coals beneath and on top of it. If you're using an oven, preheat it to 425°F (220°C).
2. In a large mixing bowl, whisk together the flour, salt, and sugar for the crust.
3. Add the cold cubed butter to the flour mixture. Use a pastry cutter or your fingers to cut the butter into the flour until the mixture resembles coarse crumbs.
4. Gradually add the ice water, 1 tablespoon at a time, mixing with a fork until the dough comes together. Be careful not to overwork the dough.
5. Shape the dough into a disk, wrap it in plastic wrap, and refrigerate it for at least 30 minutes.
6. Once chilled, roll out the dough on a floured surface to fit the bottom and sides of your greased Dutch oven.
7. Press the dough into the bottom and up the sides of the Dutch oven, trimming any excess if necessary. Use a fork to prick holes in the bottom of the crust.

8. In a separate mixing bowl, whisk together the pumpkin puree, sweetened condensed milk, eggs, spices, and salt until well combined.
9. Pour the pumpkin filling into the prepared crust in the Dutch oven.
10. Cover the Dutch oven with its lid and place it over the preheated coals. If using an oven, place the Dutch oven on a baking sheet and bake for about 15 minutes.
11. Reduce the heat to 350°F (175°C) and continue baking for another 35-40 minutes, or until the filling is set and the crust is golden brown.
12. Once done, remove the Dutch oven from the heat or oven and let the pumpkin pie cool completely before slicing and serving.
13. Serve slices of the Dutch Oven Pumpkin Pie with whipped cream or vanilla ice cream on top, if desired. Enjoy the warm and comforting flavors of fall!

Dutch Oven Cinnamon Rolls

Ingredients:

For the dough:

- 4 cups all-purpose flour
- 1/4 cup granulated sugar
- 1 teaspoon salt
- 1 package (2 1/4 teaspoons) active dry yeast
- 1 cup milk
- 1/4 cup unsalted butter, melted
- 2 large eggs

For the filling:

- 1/2 cup unsalted butter, softened
- 1 cup brown sugar, packed
- 2 tablespoons ground cinnamon

For the icing:

- 1 cup powdered sugar
- 2 tablespoons milk
- 1/2 teaspoon vanilla extract

Instructions:

1. In a large mixing bowl, combine 2 cups of flour, granulated sugar, salt, and yeast.
2. In a saucepan, heat the milk until it's warm but not boiling. Add the melted butter to the warm milk.
3. Pour the milk and butter mixture into the dry ingredients, and then add the eggs. Stir until well combined.
4. Gradually add the remaining 2 cups of flour, stirring until the dough comes together.
5. Turn the dough out onto a floured surface and knead it for about 5-7 minutes, or until it becomes smooth and elastic.

6. Place the dough in a greased bowl, cover it with a clean kitchen towel, and let it rise in a warm place for about 1 hour, or until it doubles in size.
7. Punch down the risen dough and roll it out into a large rectangle, about 1/4 inch thick.
8. Spread the softened butter evenly over the dough rectangle, leaving a small border around the edges.
9. In a small bowl, mix together the brown sugar and cinnamon for the filling. Sprinkle this mixture evenly over the buttered dough.
10. Starting from one long edge, tightly roll up the dough into a log.
11. Use a sharp knife to slice the log into 12 equal-sized rolls.
12. Grease the bottom and sides of your Dutch oven with butter or cooking spray.
13. Arrange the cinnamon rolls in the Dutch oven, leaving a little space between each one.
14. Cover the Dutch oven with its lid and let the rolls rise for another 30-45 minutes, or until they've doubled in size.
15. Preheat your Dutch oven by placing coals beneath and on top of it. If you're using an oven, preheat it to 350°F (175°C).
16. Once the rolls have risen, place the Dutch oven over the preheated coals or in the oven and bake for about 25-30 minutes, or until the rolls are golden brown and cooked through.
17. While the rolls are baking, prepare the icing by mixing together the powdered sugar, milk, and vanilla extract until smooth.
18. Once the rolls are done, remove them from the Dutch oven and drizzle the icing over the top while they're still warm.
19. Serve the Dutch Oven Cinnamon Rolls warm and enjoy their deliciously sweet and gooey goodness!

Dutch Oven S'mores Dip

Ingredients:

- 1 bag (12 ounces) of chocolate chips
- 1 bag (10 ounces) of marshmallows
- Graham crackers, for dipping

Instructions:

1. Preheat your Dutch oven by placing coals beneath and on top of it. If you're using an oven, preheat it to 350°F (175°C).
2. Pour the chocolate chips into the bottom of the Dutch oven, spreading them out evenly.
3. Arrange the marshmallows on top of the chocolate chips, covering them completely.
4. Cover the Dutch oven with its lid and place it over the preheated coals. If using an oven, place the Dutch oven on a baking sheet and bake for about 10-15 minutes, or until the marshmallows are golden brown and melted.
5. Once done, remove the Dutch oven from the heat or oven.
6. Serve the S'mores Dip directly from the Dutch oven, and use graham crackers to scoop up the melted chocolate and marshmallows.
7. Enjoy the gooey and decadent S'mores Dip with friends and family around the campfire or at home!

Dutch Oven Pear Tart

Ingredients:

For the crust:

- 1 1/4 cups all-purpose flour
- 1/4 cup granulated sugar
- 1/2 cup unsalted butter, cold and cut into small pieces
- 1 egg yolk
- 2 tablespoons cold water

For the filling:

- 4-5 ripe pears, peeled, cored, and thinly sliced
- 1/4 cup granulated sugar
- 1 tablespoon lemon juice
- 1 teaspoon ground cinnamon
- 1/4 teaspoon ground nutmeg

For the glaze:

- 1/4 cup apricot preserves
- 1 tablespoon water

Instructions:

1. Preheat your Dutch oven by placing coals beneath and on top of it. If you're using an oven, preheat it to 375°F (190°C).
2. In a large mixing bowl, combine the flour and sugar for the crust. Add the cold butter pieces and use a pastry cutter or your fingers to cut the butter into the flour mixture until it resembles coarse crumbs.
3. In a small bowl, whisk together the egg yolk and cold water. Gradually add the egg mixture to the flour mixture, stirring until the dough comes together. Shape

the dough into a disk, wrap it in plastic wrap, and refrigerate it for at least 30 minutes.
4. In another mixing bowl, toss the sliced pears with granulated sugar, lemon juice, cinnamon, and nutmeg until well coated.
5. Roll out the chilled dough on a floured surface to fit the bottom and sides of your greased Dutch oven.
6. Press the dough into the bottom and up the sides of the Dutch oven, trimming any excess if necessary.
7. Arrange the sliced pears in an even layer over the crust in the Dutch oven.
8. Cover the Dutch oven with its lid and place it over the preheated coals. If using an oven, place the Dutch oven on a baking sheet and bake for about 25-30 minutes, or until the crust is golden brown and the pears are tender.
9. While the tart is baking, prepare the glaze by heating the apricot preserves and water in a small saucepan over medium heat until melted and smooth.
10. Once the tart is done, remove it from the heat or oven and let it cool slightly.
11. Brush the warm tart with the apricot glaze.
12. Serve the Dutch Oven Pear Tart warm or at room temperature, optionally with a scoop of vanilla ice cream or a dollop of whipped cream on top. Enjoy the delicious combination of sweet pears and buttery crust!

Dutch Oven Raspberry Swirl Cheesecake

Ingredients:

For the crust:

- 1 1/2 cups graham cracker crumbs
- 1/4 cup granulated sugar
- 1/2 cup unsalted butter, melted

For the raspberry swirl:

- 1 cup fresh raspberries
- 2 tablespoons granulated sugar

For the cheesecake filling:

- 3 packages (8 ounces each) cream cheese, softened
- 1 cup granulated sugar
- 1 teaspoon vanilla extract
- 3 large eggs
- 1/4 cup sour cream
- 1/4 cup heavy cream

Instructions:

1. Preheat your Dutch oven by placing coals beneath and on top of it. If you're using an oven, preheat it to 325°F (160°C).
2. In a mixing bowl, combine the graham cracker crumbs, granulated sugar, and melted butter for the crust. Mix until well combined.
3. Press the crust mixture evenly into the bottom of your greased Dutch oven.
4. In a small saucepan, heat the raspberries and granulated sugar over medium heat, stirring occasionally, until the raspberries break down and release their

juices. Remove from heat and strain the mixture through a fine mesh sieve to remove the seeds. Set aside.
5. In a large mixing bowl, beat the softened cream cheese until smooth and creamy.
6. Add the granulated sugar and vanilla extract to the cream cheese, and beat until well combined.
7. Add the eggs one at a time, beating well after each addition.
8. Stir in the sour cream and heavy cream until smooth.
9. Pour the cheesecake filling over the prepared crust in the Dutch oven, spreading it out evenly.
10. Drizzle the raspberry sauce over the cheesecake filling in the Dutch oven.
11. Use a knife or skewer to gently swirl the raspberry sauce into the cheesecake filling, creating a marbled effect.
12. Cover the Dutch oven with its lid and place it over the preheated coals. If using an oven, place the Dutch oven on a baking sheet and bake for about 45-55 minutes, or until the edges are set and the center is slightly jiggly.
13. Once done, remove the Dutch oven from the heat or oven and let the cheesecake cool completely.
14. Once cooled, refrigerate the cheesecake for at least 4 hours or overnight to set.
15. Serve the Dutch Oven Raspberry Swirl Cheesecake chilled, optionally with fresh raspberries or whipped cream on top. Enjoy this creamy and tangy dessert with a delightful raspberry twist!

Dutch Oven Apricot Cobbler

Ingredients:

For the apricot filling:

- 6 cups fresh apricots, pitted and halved
- 1/2 cup granulated sugar
- 1 tablespoon lemon juice
- 2 tablespoons cornstarch
- 1/2 teaspoon vanilla extract

For the cobbler topping:

- 1 cup all-purpose flour
- 1/2 cup granulated sugar
- 1 teaspoon baking powder
- 1/4 teaspoon salt
- 1/2 cup unsalted butter, melted
- 1/4 cup milk
- 1 teaspoon vanilla extract

Instructions:

1. Preheat your Dutch oven by placing coals beneath and on top of it. If you're using an oven, preheat it to 375°F (190°C).
2. In a large mixing bowl, combine the apricots, granulated sugar, lemon juice, cornstarch, and vanilla extract for the filling. Stir until the apricots are well coated. Set aside.
3. In another mixing bowl, whisk together the flour, sugar, baking powder, and salt for the cobbler topping.
4. Stir in the melted butter, milk, and vanilla extract until the mixture forms a thick batter.
5. Pour the apricot filling into the bottom of your greased Dutch oven, spreading it out evenly.

6. Drop spoonfuls of the cobbler batter over the apricot filling in the Dutch oven, covering it as much as possible.
7. Cover the Dutch oven with its lid and place it over the preheated coals. If using an oven, place the Dutch oven on a baking sheet and bake for about 35-40 minutes, or until the cobbler topping is golden brown and cooked through, and the apricot filling is bubbly.
8. Once done, remove the Dutch oven from the heat or oven and let the apricot cobbler cool slightly.
9. Serve the Dutch Oven Apricot Cobbler warm, optionally with a scoop of vanilla ice cream or a dollop of whipped cream on top. Enjoy the sweet and tangy flavors of this delightful dessert!

Dutch Oven Fig and Walnut Cake

Ingredients:

For the cake:

- 1 1/2 cups all-purpose flour
- 1 teaspoon baking powder
- 1/2 teaspoon baking soda
- 1/4 teaspoon salt
- 1/2 cup unsalted butter, softened
- 3/4 cup granulated sugar
- 2 large eggs
- 1 teaspoon vanilla extract
- 1/2 cup buttermilk
- 1 cup chopped dried figs
- 1/2 cup chopped walnuts

For the glaze:

- 1/2 cup powdered sugar
- 1-2 tablespoons milk
- 1/2 teaspoon vanilla extract

Instructions:

1. Preheat your Dutch oven by placing coals beneath and on top of it. If you're using an oven, preheat it to 350°F (175°C).
2. In a mixing bowl, sift together the flour, baking powder, baking soda, and salt. Set aside.
3. In another mixing bowl, cream together the softened butter and granulated sugar until light and fluffy.
4. Beat in the eggs, one at a time, followed by the vanilla extract.
5. Gradually add the dry ingredients to the wet ingredients, alternating with the buttermilk, until everything is well combined and you have a smooth batter.

6. Fold in the chopped dried figs and walnuts until evenly distributed throughout the batter.
7. Grease the bottom and sides of your Dutch oven with butter or cooking spray.
8. Pour the batter into the greased Dutch oven, spreading it out evenly.
9. Cover the Dutch oven with its lid and place it over the preheated coals. If using an oven, place the Dutch oven on a baking sheet and bake for about 30-35 minutes, or until a toothpick inserted into the center of the cake comes out clean.
10. Once the cake is done, remove it from the heat or oven and let it cool slightly.
11. While the cake is cooling, prepare the glaze by whisking together the powdered sugar, milk, and vanilla extract until smooth. Add more milk if needed to reach your desired consistency.
12. Drizzle the glaze over the warm cake in the Dutch oven.
13. Let the cake cool completely before slicing and serving. Enjoy the rich and nutty flavors of this Dutch Oven Fig and Walnut Cake!

Dutch Oven Blackberry Cobbler

Ingredients:

For the blackberry filling:

- 6 cups fresh blackberries
- 3/4 cup granulated sugar
- 2 tablespoons cornstarch
- 1 tablespoon lemon juice
- Zest of 1 lemon

For the cobbler topping:

- 1 cup all-purpose flour
- 1/2 cup granulated sugar
- 1 teaspoon baking powder
- 1/4 teaspoon salt
- 1/2 cup unsalted butter, melted
- 1/4 cup milk
- 1 teaspoon vanilla extract

Instructions:

1. Preheat your Dutch oven by placing coals beneath and on top of it. If you're using an oven, preheat it to 375°F (190°C).
2. In a large mixing bowl, combine the blackberries, granulated sugar, cornstarch, lemon juice, and lemon zest for the filling. Toss gently until the blackberries are well coated.
3. In another mixing bowl, whisk together the flour, sugar, baking powder, and salt for the cobbler topping.
4. Stir in the melted butter, milk, and vanilla extract until the mixture forms a thick batter.
5. Pour the blackberry filling into the bottom of your greased Dutch oven, spreading it out evenly.

6. Drop spoonfuls of the cobbler batter over the blackberry filling in the Dutch oven, covering it as much as possible.
7. Cover the Dutch oven with its lid and place it over the preheated coals. If using an oven, place the Dutch oven on a baking sheet and bake for about 35-40 minutes, or until the cobbler topping is golden brown and cooked through, and the blackberry filling is bubbly.
8. Once done, remove the Dutch oven from the heat or oven and let the blackberry cobbler cool slightly.
9. Serve the Dutch Oven Blackberry Cobbler warm, optionally with a scoop of vanilla ice cream or a dollop of whipped cream on top. Enjoy the sweet and tangy flavors of this classic dessert!

Dutch Oven Plum Clafoutis

Ingredients:

- 1 tablespoon unsalted butter, softened (for greasing the Dutch oven)
- 4 cups ripe plums, pitted and halved
- 1/2 cup granulated sugar, divided
- 3 large eggs
- 1 cup whole milk
- 1/2 cup all-purpose flour
- 1 teaspoon vanilla extract
- 1/4 teaspoon salt
- Powdered sugar, for dusting

Instructions:

1. Preheat your Dutch oven by placing coals beneath and on top of it. If you're using an oven, preheat it to 350°F (175°C).
2. Grease the bottom and sides of your Dutch oven with softened butter.
3. Arrange the halved plums in a single layer on the bottom of the Dutch oven.
4. Sprinkle half of the granulated sugar (1/4 cup) over the plums.
5. In a mixing bowl, whisk together the eggs, remaining granulated sugar (1/4 cup), whole milk, flour, vanilla extract, and salt until smooth and well combined.
6. Pour the batter over the plums in the Dutch oven, making sure to cover them evenly.
7. Cover the Dutch oven with its lid and place it over the preheated coals. If using an oven, place the Dutch oven on a baking sheet and bake for about 40-45 minutes, or until the clafoutis is set and golden brown on top.
8. Once done, remove the Dutch oven from the heat or oven and let the plum clafoutis cool slightly.
9. Dust the top of the clafoutis with powdered sugar before serving.
10. Serve the Dutch Oven Plum Clafoutis warm or at room temperature. Enjoy the sweet and juicy flavors of this classic French dessert!

Dutch Oven Orange Pound Cake

Ingredients:

For the cake:

- 1 1/2 cups all-purpose flour
- 1 teaspoon baking powder
- 1/4 teaspoon salt
- 1/2 cup unsalted butter, softened
- 1 cup granulated sugar
- 3 large eggs
- 1/2 cup sour cream
- 1 tablespoon orange zest
- 1/4 cup freshly squeezed orange juice
- 1 teaspoon vanilla extract

For the glaze:

- 1 cup powdered sugar
- 2-3 tablespoons freshly squeezed orange juice
- Additional orange zest for garnish (optional)

Instructions:

1. Preheat your Dutch oven by placing coals beneath and on top of it. If you're using an oven, preheat it to 350°F (175°C).
2. Grease the bottom and sides of your Dutch oven with butter or cooking spray.
3. In a mixing bowl, whisk together the flour, baking powder, and salt. Set aside.
4. In another mixing bowl, cream together the softened butter and granulated sugar until light and fluffy.
5. Beat in the eggs, one at a time, until well incorporated.
6. Stir in the sour cream, orange zest, orange juice, and vanilla extract until smooth.
7. Gradually add the dry ingredients to the wet ingredients, mixing until just combined. Be careful not to overmix.
8. Pour the batter into the greased Dutch oven, spreading it out evenly.

9. Cover the Dutch oven with its lid and place it over the preheated coals. If using an oven, place the Dutch oven on a baking sheet and bake for about 45-50 minutes, or until a toothpick inserted into the center of the cake comes out clean.
10. Once the cake is done, remove it from the heat or oven and let it cool slightly in the Dutch oven.
11. While the cake is cooling, prepare the glaze by whisking together the powdered sugar and orange juice until smooth. Add more orange juice if needed to reach your desired consistency.
12. Drizzle the glaze over the warm cake in the Dutch oven.
13. If desired, garnish the cake with additional orange zest for extra flavor and presentation.
14. Let the cake cool completely before slicing and serving. Enjoy the moist and citrusy flavors of this Dutch Oven Orange Pound Cake!

Dutch Oven Pecan Pie

Ingredients:

For the pie crust:

- 1 1/4 cups all-purpose flour
- 1/2 teaspoon salt
- 1/2 cup unsalted butter, cold and cut into small pieces
- 2-4 tablespoons ice water

For the pecan pie filling:

- 1 cup light corn syrup
- 3/4 cup granulated sugar
- 3 large eggs
- 2 tablespoons unsalted butter, melted
- 1 teaspoon vanilla extract
- 1 1/2 cups pecan halves

Instructions:

1. Preheat your Dutch oven by placing coals beneath and on top of it. If you're using an oven, preheat it to 350°F (175°C).
2. In a large mixing bowl, whisk together the flour and salt for the pie crust.
3. Add the cold butter pieces to the flour mixture. Use a pastry cutter or your fingers to cut the butter into the flour until the mixture resembles coarse crumbs.
4. Gradually add the ice water, 1 tablespoon at a time, mixing with a fork until the dough comes together. Be careful not to overwork the dough.
5. Shape the dough into a disk, wrap it in plastic wrap, and refrigerate it for at least 30 minutes.
6. Once chilled, roll out the dough on a floured surface to fit the bottom and sides of your greased Dutch oven.
7. Press the dough into the bottom and up the sides of the Dutch oven, trimming any excess if necessary.

8. In a mixing bowl, whisk together the corn syrup, granulated sugar, eggs, melted butter, and vanilla extract until well combined.
9. Stir in the pecan halves until evenly distributed.
10. Pour the pecan pie filling into the prepared pie crust in the Dutch oven.
11. Cover the Dutch oven with its lid and place it over the preheated coals. If using an oven, place the Dutch oven on a baking sheet and bake for about 40-45 minutes, or until the filling is set and the crust is golden brown.
12. Once done, remove the Dutch oven from the heat or oven and let the pecan pie cool completely before slicing and serving.
13. Serve the Dutch Oven Pecan Pie at room temperature or slightly warm, optionally with a dollop of whipped cream or a scoop of vanilla ice cream on top. Enjoy the rich and nutty flavors of this classic dessert!

Dutch Oven Cranberry Crisp

Ingredients:

For the cranberry filling:

- 4 cups fresh cranberries
- 3/4 cup granulated sugar
- Zest and juice of 1 orange
- 1 tablespoon cornstarch

For the crisp topping:

- 1 cup old-fashioned oats
- 1/2 cup all-purpose flour
- 1/2 cup brown sugar
- 1/2 teaspoon ground cinnamon
- 1/4 teaspoon salt
- 1/2 cup unsalted butter, melted

Instructions:

1. Preheat your Dutch oven by placing coals beneath and on top of it. If you're using an oven, preheat it to 350°F (175°C).
2. In a mixing bowl, combine the fresh cranberries, granulated sugar, orange zest, orange juice, and cornstarch. Toss until the cranberries are well coated.
3. Pour the cranberry mixture into the bottom of your greased Dutch oven, spreading it out evenly.
4. In another mixing bowl, combine the oats, flour, brown sugar, cinnamon, and salt for the crisp topping.
5. Stir in the melted butter until the mixture is crumbly and evenly moistened.
6. Sprinkle the crisp topping over the cranberry filling in the Dutch oven, covering it as much as possible.
7. Cover the Dutch oven with its lid and place it over the preheated coals. If using an oven, place the Dutch oven on a baking sheet and bake for about 35-40 minutes,

or until the cranberry filling is bubbling and the crisp topping is golden brown and crisp.
8. Once done, remove the Dutch oven from the heat or oven and let the cranberry crisp cool slightly.
9. Serve the Dutch Oven Cranberry Crisp warm, optionally with a scoop of vanilla ice cream or a dollop of whipped cream on top. Enjoy the sweet and tart flavors of this delightful dessert!

Dutch Oven Rhubarb Crumble

Ingredients:

For the rhubarb filling:

- 6 cups chopped rhubarb
- 1 cup granulated sugar
- 2 tablespoons cornstarch
- Zest and juice of 1 orange

For the crumble topping:

- 1 cup old-fashioned oats
- 1/2 cup all-purpose flour
- 1/2 cup packed brown sugar
- 1/2 teaspoon ground cinnamon
- 1/4 teaspoon salt
- 1/2 cup unsalted butter, melted

Instructions:

1. Preheat your Dutch oven by placing coals beneath and on top of it. If you're using an oven, preheat it to 375°F (190°C).
2. In a mixing bowl, combine the chopped rhubarb, granulated sugar, cornstarch, orange zest, and orange juice. Toss until the rhubarb is well coated.
3. Pour the rhubarb mixture into the bottom of your greased Dutch oven, spreading it out evenly.
4. In another mixing bowl, combine the oats, flour, brown sugar, cinnamon, and salt for the crumble topping.
5. Stir in the melted butter until the mixture is crumbly and evenly moistened.
6. Sprinkle the crumble topping over the rhubarb filling in the Dutch oven, covering it as much as possible.
7. Cover the Dutch oven with its lid and place it over the preheated coals. If using an oven, place the Dutch oven on a baking sheet and bake for about 40-45 minutes,

or until the rhubarb filling is bubbling and the crumble topping is golden brown and crisp.
8. Once done, remove the Dutch oven from the heat or oven and let the rhubarb crumble cool slightly.
9. Serve the Dutch Oven Rhubarb Crumble warm, optionally with a scoop of vanilla ice cream or a dollop of whipped cream on top. Enjoy the sweet and tangy flavors of this delightful dessert!

Dutch Oven Coconut Macaroons

Ingredients:

- 4 large egg whites
- 1/2 cup granulated sugar
- 1 teaspoon vanilla extract
- 1/4 teaspoon almond extract (optional)
- 3 cups sweetened shredded coconut
- Pinch of salt

Instructions:

1. Preheat your Dutch oven by placing coals beneath and on top of it. If you're using an oven, preheat it to 325°F (160°C).
2. In a heatproof mixing bowl, whisk together the egg whites, granulated sugar, vanilla extract, and almond extract (if using).
3. Place the bowl over a pot of simmering water (creating a double boiler) and whisk continuously until the sugar is dissolved and the mixture is warm to the touch, about 2-3 minutes. Be careful not to cook the egg whites.
4. Remove the bowl from the heat and stir in the shredded coconut and a pinch of salt until well combined.
5. Line a baking sheet with parchment paper.
6. Using a spoon or a cookie scoop, portion the coconut mixture into small mounds and place them on the prepared baking sheet, leaving some space between each macaroon.
7. Grease the bottom and sides of your Dutch oven with butter or cooking spray.
8. Arrange the macaroons in the Dutch oven, making sure they fit in a single layer.
9. Cover the Dutch oven with its lid and place it over the preheated coals. If using an oven, place the Dutch oven on a baking sheet and bake for about 15-20 minutes, or until the macaroons are lightly golden brown on the outside and set.
10. Once done, remove the Dutch oven from the heat or oven and let the coconut macaroons cool completely before serving.
11. Serve the Dutch Oven Coconut Macaroons at room temperature. Enjoy the chewy and sweet coconut goodness!

Dutch Oven Espresso Brownies

Ingredients:

- 1/2 cup unsalted butter
- 1 cup granulated sugar
- 2 large eggs
- 1 teaspoon vanilla extract
- 1 tablespoon instant espresso powder
- 1/3 cup unsweetened cocoa powder
- 1/2 cup all-purpose flour
- 1/4 teaspoon salt
- 1/4 teaspoon baking powder
- 1/2 cup semisweet chocolate chips (optional)
- Powdered sugar, for dusting (optional)

Instructions:

1. Preheat your Dutch oven by placing coals beneath and on top of it. If you're using an oven, preheat it to 350°F (175°C).
2. In a microwave-safe bowl, melt the butter in the microwave.
3. In a mixing bowl, whisk together the melted butter and granulated sugar until well combined.
4. Add the eggs and vanilla extract to the butter mixture, and whisk until smooth.
5. Stir in the instant espresso powder until dissolved.
6. Sift in the cocoa powder, all-purpose flour, salt, and baking powder into the wet ingredients. Mix until just combined. Do not overmix.
7. If using, fold in the semisweet chocolate chips until evenly distributed throughout the batter.
8. Grease the bottom and sides of your Dutch oven with butter or cooking spray.
9. Pour the brownie batter into the greased Dutch oven, spreading it out evenly.
10. Cover the Dutch oven with its lid and place it over the preheated coals. If using an oven, place the Dutch oven on a baking sheet and bake for about 25-30 minutes, or until a toothpick inserted into the center comes out with a few moist crumbs.
11. Once done, remove the Dutch oven from the heat or oven and let the espresso brownies cool slightly.
12. If desired, dust the top of the brownies with powdered sugar before serving.

13. Serve the Dutch Oven Espresso Brownies warm or at room temperature. Enjoy the rich and intense flavors of these decadent treats!

Dutch Oven Almond Cake

Ingredients:

- 1 cup all-purpose flour
- 1 teaspoon baking powder
- 1/4 teaspoon salt
- 1/2 cup unsalted butter, softened
- 3/4 cup granulated sugar
- 2 large eggs
- 1 teaspoon almond extract
- 1/3 cup milk
- 1/2 cup almond meal (ground almonds)
- Sliced almonds, for topping (optional)
- Powdered sugar, for dusting (optional)

Instructions:

1. Preheat your Dutch oven by placing coals beneath and on top of it. If you're using an oven, preheat it to 350°F (175°C).
2. Grease the bottom and sides of your Dutch oven with butter or cooking spray.
3. In a mixing bowl, sift together the all-purpose flour, baking powder, and salt. Set aside.
4. In another mixing bowl, cream together the softened butter and granulated sugar until light and fluffy.
5. Beat in the eggs, one at a time, until well incorporated.
6. Stir in the almond extract.
7. Gradually add the dry ingredients to the wet ingredients, alternating with the milk, and mixing until just combined.
8. Fold in the almond meal until evenly distributed throughout the batter.
9. Pour the batter into the greased Dutch oven, spreading it out evenly.
10. If desired, sprinkle sliced almonds over the top of the cake batter.
11. Cover the Dutch oven with its lid and place it over the preheated coals. If using an oven, place the Dutch oven on a baking sheet and bake for about 30-35 minutes, or until a toothpick inserted into the center of the cake comes out clean.
12. Once done, remove the Dutch oven from the heat or oven and let the almond cake cool slightly.

13. If desired, dust the top of the cake with powdered sugar before serving.
14. Serve the Dutch Oven Almond Cake warm or at room temperature. Enjoy the moist and nutty flavors of this delightful dessert!

Dutch Oven Gingerbread

Ingredients:

- 1/2 cup unsalted butter, melted
- 1/2 cup granulated sugar
- 1/2 cup molasses
- 1 large egg
- 1 teaspoon vanilla extract
- 1 cup all-purpose flour
- 1/2 teaspoon baking soda
- 1/2 teaspoon ground cinnamon
- 1/2 teaspoon ground ginger
- 1/4 teaspoon ground cloves
- 1/4 teaspoon salt
- 1/2 cup hot water

Instructions:

1. Preheat your Dutch oven by placing coals beneath and on top of it. If you're using an oven, preheat it to 350°F (175°C).
2. Grease the bottom and sides of your Dutch oven with butter or cooking spray.
3. In a mixing bowl, whisk together the melted butter, granulated sugar, molasses, egg, and vanilla extract until well combined.
4. In another mixing bowl, sift together the all-purpose flour, baking soda, ground cinnamon, ground ginger, ground cloves, and salt.
5. Gradually add the dry ingredients to the wet ingredients, mixing until just combined.
6. Stir in the hot water until the batter is smooth.
7. Pour the batter into the greased Dutch oven, spreading it out evenly.
8. Cover the Dutch oven with its lid and place it over the preheated coals. If using an oven, place the Dutch oven on a baking sheet and bake for about 30-35 minutes, or until a toothpick inserted into the center of the gingerbread comes out clean.
9. Once done, remove the Dutch oven from the heat or oven and let the gingerbread cool slightly.
10. Serve the Dutch Oven Gingerbread warm or at room temperature. Enjoy the warm and comforting flavors of this classic dessert!

Dutch Oven Date Bars

Ingredients:

For the date filling:

- 2 cups pitted dates, chopped
- 1 cup water
- 1/4 cup granulated sugar
- 1 teaspoon lemon juice
- 1/2 teaspoon vanilla extract

For the oatmeal crust and topping:

- 1 1/2 cups old-fashioned oats
- 1 cup all-purpose flour
- 1/2 cup packed brown sugar
- 1/4 teaspoon baking soda
- 1/4 teaspoon salt
- 1/2 cup unsalted butter, melted

Instructions:

1. Preheat your Dutch oven by placing coals beneath and on top of it. If you're using an oven, preheat it to 350°F (175°C).
2. Grease the bottom and sides of your Dutch oven with butter or cooking spray.
3. In a medium saucepan, combine the chopped dates, water, granulated sugar, lemon juice, and vanilla extract for the date filling.
4. Bring the mixture to a boil over medium-high heat, then reduce the heat to low and simmer, stirring occasionally, for about 10-15 minutes or until the dates are soft and the mixture has thickened. Remove from heat and let cool slightly.
5. In a mixing bowl, combine the old-fashioned oats, all-purpose flour, brown sugar, baking soda, and salt for the oatmeal crust and topping.
6. Stir in the melted butter until the mixture is crumbly and well combined.
7. Press half of the oatmeal mixture into the bottom of the greased Dutch oven, forming an even layer.

8. Spread the date filling evenly over the oatmeal crust.
9. Sprinkle the remaining oatmeal mixture evenly over the date filling, forming the topping.
10. Cover the Dutch oven with its lid and place it over the preheated coals. If using an oven, place the Dutch oven on a baking sheet and bake for about 25-30 minutes, or until the oatmeal crust and topping are golden brown.
11. Once done, remove the Dutch oven from the heat or oven and let the date bars cool completely before slicing into squares.
12. Serve the Dutch Oven Date Bars at room temperature. Enjoy the sweet and chewy goodness of these delightful treats!

Dutch Oven Cherry Chocolate Chip Cookies

Ingredients:

- 1/2 cup unsalted butter, softened
- 1/2 cup granulated sugar
- 1/2 cup packed brown sugar
- 1 large egg
- 1 teaspoon vanilla extract
- 1 1/2 cups all-purpose flour
- 1/2 teaspoon baking soda
- 1/4 teaspoon salt
- 3/4 cup dried cherries, chopped
- 3/4 cup semisweet chocolate chips

Instructions:

1. Preheat your Dutch oven by placing coals beneath and on top of it. If you're using an oven, preheat it to 350°F (175°C).
2. Grease the bottom and sides of your Dutch oven with butter or cooking spray.
3. In a mixing bowl, cream together the softened butter, granulated sugar, and brown sugar until light and fluffy.
4. Beat in the egg and vanilla extract until well combined.
5. In another mixing bowl, whisk together the all-purpose flour, baking soda, and salt.
6. Gradually add the dry ingredients to the wet ingredients, mixing until just combined.
7. Stir in the chopped dried cherries and semisweet chocolate chips until evenly distributed throughout the cookie dough.
8. Drop spoonfuls of the cookie dough onto the greased Dutch oven, spacing them out evenly.
9. Cover the Dutch oven with its lid and place it over the preheated coals. If using an oven, place the Dutch oven on a baking sheet and bake for about 12-15 minutes, or until the cookies are golden brown around the edges.
10. Once done, remove the Dutch oven from the heat or oven and let the cookies cool slightly before transferring them to a wire rack to cool completely.
11. Serve the Dutch Oven Cherry Chocolate Chip Cookies at room temperature. Enjoy the sweet and tangy flavors of these delightful cookies!

Dutch Oven Butterscotch Blondies

Ingredients:

- 1/2 cup unsalted butter, melted
- 1 cup packed brown sugar
- 1 large egg
- 1 teaspoon vanilla extract
- 1 cup all-purpose flour
- 1/2 teaspoon baking powder
- 1/4 teaspoon salt
- 1/2 cup butterscotch chips

Instructions:

1. Preheat your Dutch oven by placing coals beneath and on top of it. If you're using an oven, preheat it to 350°F (175°C).
2. Grease the bottom and sides of your Dutch oven with butter or cooking spray.
3. In a mixing bowl, combine the melted butter and packed brown sugar until well mixed.
4. Beat in the egg and vanilla extract until smooth.
5. In another mixing bowl, whisk together the all-purpose flour, baking powder, and salt.
6. Gradually add the dry ingredients to the wet ingredients, stirring until just combined.
7. Fold in the butterscotch chips until evenly distributed throughout the blondie batter.
8. Spread the blondie batter evenly into the greased Dutch oven.
9. Cover the Dutch oven with its lid and place it over the preheated coals. If using an oven, place the Dutch oven on a baking sheet and bake for about 20-25 minutes, or until the blondies are golden brown and a toothpick inserted into the center comes out clean.
10. Once done, remove the Dutch oven from the heat or oven and let the blondies cool slightly before slicing into squares.
11. Serve the Dutch Oven Butterscotch Blondies warm or at room temperature. Enjoy the rich and buttery flavor of these delightful treats!

Dutch Oven Hazelnut Torte

Ingredients:

For the torte:

- 1 cup hazelnuts, toasted and finely ground
- 1/2 cup all-purpose flour
- 1 teaspoon baking powder
- 1/4 teaspoon salt
- 1/2 cup unsalted butter, softened
- 3/4 cup granulated sugar
- 3 large eggs
- 1 teaspoon vanilla extract
- 2 tablespoons milk

For the glaze:

- 1/2 cup semisweet chocolate chips
- 2 tablespoons unsalted butter
- 1 tablespoon light corn syrup
- 1 tablespoon water
- Chopped hazelnuts, for garnish (optional)

Instructions:

1. Preheat your Dutch oven by placing coals beneath and on top of it. If you're using an oven, preheat it to 350°F (175°C).
2. Grease the bottom and sides of your Dutch oven with butter or cooking spray.
3. In a mixing bowl, combine the finely ground hazelnuts, all-purpose flour, baking powder, and salt. Set aside.
4. In another mixing bowl, cream together the softened butter and granulated sugar until light and fluffy.
5. Beat in the eggs, one at a time, until well incorporated.
6. Stir in the vanilla extract.

7. Gradually add the dry ingredients to the wet ingredients, alternating with the milk, and mixing until just combined.
8. Pour the batter into the greased Dutch oven, spreading it out evenly.
9. Cover the Dutch oven with its lid and place it over the preheated coals. If using an oven, place the Dutch oven on a baking sheet and bake for about 25-30 minutes, or until a toothpick inserted into the center of the torte comes out clean.
10. Once done, remove the Dutch oven from the heat or oven and let the hazelnut torte cool slightly.
11. While the torte is cooling, prepare the glaze. In a small saucepan, combine the semisweet chocolate chips, unsalted butter, light corn syrup, and water. Cook over low heat, stirring constantly, until the chocolate chips and butter are melted and the mixture is smooth.
12. Drizzle the chocolate glaze over the warm hazelnut torte in the Dutch oven.
13. If desired, garnish the top of the torte with chopped hazelnuts for added flavor and decoration.
14. Let the hazelnut torte cool completely before slicing and serving.
15. Serve the Dutch Oven Hazelnut Torte at room temperature. Enjoy the rich and nutty flavors of this delightful dessert!

Dutch Oven Lemon Poppy Seed Cake

Ingredients:

For the cake:

- 1 1/2 cups all-purpose flour
- 2 tablespoons poppy seeds
- 1 teaspoon baking powder
- 1/2 teaspoon baking soda
- 1/4 teaspoon salt
- 1/2 cup unsalted butter, softened
- 1 cup granulated sugar
- 2 large eggs
- 1/2 cup sour cream
- Zest of 2 lemons
- 2 tablespoons freshly squeezed lemon juice
- 1 teaspoon vanilla extract

For the glaze:

- 1 cup powdered sugar
- 2-3 tablespoons freshly squeezed lemon juice

Instructions:

1. Preheat your Dutch oven by placing coals beneath and on top of it. If you're using an oven, preheat it to 350°F (175°C).
2. Grease the bottom and sides of your Dutch oven with butter or cooking spray.
3. In a mixing bowl, whisk together the all-purpose flour, poppy seeds, baking powder, baking soda, and salt. Set aside.
4. In another mixing bowl, cream together the softened butter and granulated sugar until light and fluffy.
5. Beat in the eggs, one at a time, until well incorporated.
6. Stir in the sour cream, lemon zest, lemon juice, and vanilla extract until smooth.

7. Gradually add the dry ingredients to the wet ingredients, mixing until just combined.
8. Pour the batter into the greased Dutch oven, spreading it out evenly.
9. Cover the Dutch oven with its lid and place it over the preheated coals. If using an oven, place the Dutch oven on a baking sheet and bake for about 30-35 minutes, or until a toothpick inserted into the center of the cake comes out clean.
10. Once done, remove the Dutch oven from the heat or oven and let the lemon poppy seed cake cool slightly.
11. While the cake is cooling, prepare the glaze. In a small bowl, whisk together the powdered sugar and freshly squeezed lemon juice until smooth.
12. Drizzle the glaze over the warm cake in the Dutch oven.
13. Let the cake cool completely before slicing and serving.
14. Serve the Dutch Oven Lemon Poppy Seed Cake at room temperature. Enjoy the refreshing citrus flavor and delicate texture of this delightful dessert!

Dutch Oven Oatmeal Raisin Cookies

Ingredients:

- 1 cup unsalted butter, softened
- 1 cup packed brown sugar
- 1/2 cup granulated sugar
- 2 large eggs
- 1 teaspoon vanilla extract
- 1 1/2 cups all-purpose flour
- 1 teaspoon baking soda
- 1 teaspoon ground cinnamon
- 1/2 teaspoon salt
- 3 cups old-fashioned oats
- 1 cup raisins

Instructions:

1. Preheat your Dutch oven by placing coals beneath and on top of it. If you're using an oven, preheat it to 350°F (175°C).
2. Grease the bottom and sides of your Dutch oven with butter or cooking spray.
3. In a mixing bowl, cream together the softened butter, packed brown sugar, and granulated sugar until light and fluffy.
4. Beat in the eggs, one at a time, until well incorporated.
5. Stir in the vanilla extract.
6. In another mixing bowl, whisk together the all-purpose flour, baking soda, ground cinnamon, and salt.
7. Gradually add the dry ingredients to the wet ingredients, mixing until just combined.
8. Stir in the old-fashioned oats and raisins until evenly distributed throughout the cookie dough.
9. Drop spoonfuls of the cookie dough onto the greased Dutch oven, spacing them out evenly.
10. Cover the Dutch oven with its lid and place it over the preheated coals. If using an oven, place the Dutch oven on a baking sheet and bake for about 10-12 minutes, or until the cookies are golden brown around the edges.

11. Once done, remove the Dutch oven from the heat or oven and let the oatmeal raisin cookies cool slightly before transferring them to a wire rack to cool completely.
12. Serve the Dutch Oven Oatmeal Raisin Cookies at room temperature. Enjoy the hearty and comforting flavors of these classic cookies!

Dutch Oven Peach Melba

Ingredients:

For the peaches:

- 4 ripe peaches, halved and pitted
- 1/4 cup granulated sugar
- 1 tablespoon lemon juice

For the raspberry sauce:

- 1 cup fresh raspberries
- 2 tablespoons granulated sugar
- 1 tablespoon lemon juice

For serving:

- Vanilla ice cream
- Fresh raspberries, for garnish (optional)
- Fresh mint leaves, for garnish (optional)

Instructions:

1. Preheat your Dutch oven by placing coals beneath and on top of it. If you're using an oven, preheat it to 350°F (175°C).
2. In a small bowl, toss the halved and pitted peaches with granulated sugar and lemon juice until well coated.
3. Place the peach halves, cut side down, in the greased Dutch oven.
4. Cover the Dutch oven with its lid and place it over the preheated coals. If using an oven, place the Dutch oven on a baking sheet and bake for about 20-25 minutes, or until the peaches are tender.
5. While the peaches are baking, prepare the raspberry sauce. In a small saucepan, combine the fresh raspberries, granulated sugar, and lemon juice. Cook over medium heat, stirring occasionally, until the raspberries break down and the sauce thickens slightly, about 5-7 minutes. Remove from heat and let cool.
6. Once the peaches are done baking, remove the Dutch oven from the heat or oven.

7. Serve the warm peach halves with a scoop of vanilla ice cream on top.
8. Drizzle the raspberry sauce over the peach and ice cream.
9. If desired, garnish with fresh raspberries and mint leaves for an extra pop of color and flavor.
10. Serve the Dutch Oven Peach Melba immediately and enjoy the delicious combination of warm baked peaches, cool vanilla ice cream, and tangy raspberry sauce!

Dutch Oven Pistachio Cake

Ingredients:

For the cake:

- 1 box (about 18.25 ounces) yellow cake mix
- 1 box (about 3.4 ounces) instant pistachio pudding mix
- 4 large eggs
- 1 cup water
- 1/2 cup vegetable oil
- 1/2 cup chopped pistachios (optional, for extra texture and flavor)

For the glaze:

- 1 cup powdered sugar
- 2-3 tablespoons milk
- 1/2 teaspoon vanilla extract
- Chopped pistachios, for garnish (optional)

Instructions:

1. Preheat your Dutch oven by placing coals beneath and on top of it. If you're using an oven, preheat it to 350°F (175°C).
2. Grease the bottom and sides of your Dutch oven with butter or cooking spray.
3. In a large mixing bowl, combine the yellow cake mix, instant pistachio pudding mix, eggs, water, and vegetable oil. Mix until well combined and smooth.
4. If desired, fold in the chopped pistachios until evenly distributed throughout the cake batter.
5. Pour the cake batter into the greased Dutch oven, spreading it out evenly.
6. Cover the Dutch oven with its lid and place it over the preheated coals. If using an oven, place the Dutch oven on a baking sheet and bake for about 30-35 minutes, or until a toothpick inserted into the center of the cake comes out clean.
7. Once done, remove the Dutch oven from the heat or oven and let the pistachio cake cool slightly.

8. While the cake is cooling, prepare the glaze. In a small bowl, whisk together the powdered sugar, milk, and vanilla extract until smooth.
9. Drizzle the glaze over the warm pistachio cake in the Dutch oven.
10. If desired, garnish the top of the cake with chopped pistachios for added texture and flavor.
11. Let the cake cool completely before slicing and serving.
12. Serve the Dutch Oven Pistachio Cake at room temperature. Enjoy the moist and flavorful pistachio goodness!

Dutch Oven Raspberry Chocolate Tart

Ingredients:

For the crust:

- 1 1/2 cups all-purpose flour
- 1/4 cup granulated sugar
- 1/4 teaspoon salt
- 1/2 cup unsalted butter, chilled and diced
- 1 large egg yolk
- 2 tablespoons ice water

For the filling:

- 1 cup semisweet chocolate chips
- 1/2 cup heavy cream
- 1 teaspoon vanilla extract

For the topping:

- 1 1/2 cups fresh raspberries
- 1 tablespoon powdered sugar, for dusting

Instructions:

1. Preheat your Dutch oven by placing coals beneath and on top of it. If you're using an oven, preheat it to 350°F (175°C).
2. In a food processor, combine the all-purpose flour, granulated sugar, and salt. Pulse to mix.
3. Add the chilled and diced unsalted butter to the flour mixture. Pulse until the mixture resembles coarse crumbs.
4. In a small bowl, whisk together the egg yolk and ice water. Gradually add the egg mixture to the flour mixture, pulsing until the dough comes together.
5. Turn the dough out onto a lightly floured surface and knead briefly until smooth.
6. Press the dough evenly into the bottom and up the sides of a greased Dutch oven to form the crust.

7. In a small saucepan, heat the heavy cream over medium heat until it just begins to simmer. Remove from heat and pour over the semisweet chocolate chips in a heatproof bowl. Let sit for 1-2 minutes, then stir until smooth and well combined. Stir in the vanilla extract.
8. Pour the chocolate ganache filling into the prepared crust in the Dutch oven, spreading it out evenly.
9. Arrange the fresh raspberries on top of the chocolate ganache filling.
10. Cover the Dutch oven with its lid and place it over the preheated coals. If using an oven, place the Dutch oven on a baking sheet and bake for about 25-30 minutes, or until the crust is golden brown.
11. Once done, remove the Dutch oven from the heat or oven and let the raspberry chocolate tart cool slightly.
12. Dust the top of the tart with powdered sugar before serving.
13. Serve the Dutch Oven Raspberry Chocolate Tart warm or at room temperature. Enjoy the decadent combination of rich chocolate and tart raspberries!

Dutch Oven Snickerdoodle Bars

Ingredients:

For the bars:

- 2 1/3 cups all-purpose flour
- 1 teaspoon baking powder
- 1/2 teaspoon salt
- 1 cup unsalted butter, softened
- 1 1/4 cups granulated sugar
- 1/2 cup packed brown sugar
- 3 large eggs
- 1 teaspoon vanilla extract

For the cinnamon sugar topping:

- 2 tablespoons granulated sugar
- 2 teaspoons ground cinnamon

Instructions:

1. Preheat your Dutch oven by placing coals beneath and on top of it. If you're using an oven, preheat it to 350°F (175°C).
2. Grease the bottom and sides of your Dutch oven with butter or cooking spray.
3. In a mixing bowl, whisk together the all-purpose flour, baking powder, and salt. Set aside.
4. In another mixing bowl, cream together the softened butter, granulated sugar, and brown sugar until light and fluffy.
5. Beat in the eggs, one at a time, until well incorporated.
6. Stir in the vanilla extract.
7. Gradually add the dry ingredients to the wet ingredients, mixing until just combined.
8. Spread the batter evenly into the greased Dutch oven.
9. In a small bowl, mix together the granulated sugar and ground cinnamon for the cinnamon sugar topping.
10. Sprinkle the cinnamon sugar mixture evenly over the top of the batter in the Dutch oven.

11. Cover the Dutch oven with its lid and place it over the preheated coals. If using an oven, place the Dutch oven on a baking sheet and bake for about 25-30 minutes, or until the bars are golden brown and a toothpick inserted into the center comes out clean.
12. Once done, remove the Dutch oven from the heat or oven and let the snickerdoodle bars cool slightly.
13. Cut the bars into squares and serve warm or at room temperature.
14. Enjoy the Dutch Oven Snickerdoodle Bars with a glass of milk or your favorite hot beverage!

Dutch Oven Tiramisu

Ingredients:

- 1 package ladyfinger cookies
- 1 cup brewed coffee, cooled
- 1/4 cup coffee liqueur (optional)
- 1 cup mascarpone cheese
- 1/2 cup powdered sugar
- 1 cup heavy cream
- Cocoa powder, for dusting

Instructions:

1. In a shallow dish, combine the cooled brewed coffee and coffee liqueur (if using).
2. Dip each ladyfinger cookie into the coffee mixture, ensuring they are soaked but not overly soggy.
3. Arrange a layer of soaked ladyfinger cookies at the bottom of the greased Dutch oven.
4. In a mixing bowl, beat the mascarpone cheese and powdered sugar until smooth and creamy.
5. In a separate mixing bowl, whip the heavy cream until stiff peaks form.
6. Gently fold the whipped cream into the mascarpone mixture until well combined.
7. Spread half of the mascarpone mixture over the layer of soaked ladyfinger cookies in the Dutch oven.
8. Repeat the process with another layer of soaked ladyfinger cookies and the remaining mascarpone mixture.
9. Cover the Dutch oven with its lid and refrigerate the tiramisu for at least 4 hours, or overnight, to allow the flavors to meld and the dessert to set.
10. Before serving, dust the top of the tiramisu with cocoa powder.
11. Serve the Dutch Oven Tiramisu chilled, and enjoy the creamy and indulgent flavors of this classic Italian dessert!

This version skips the use of raw eggs, which are traditionally found in tiramisu, for safety reasons. Additionally, the Dutch oven provides a convenient vessel for assembling and chilling the dessert.

Dutch Oven Upside-Down Pear Cake

Ingredients:

For the pear topping:

- 3 ripe but firm pears, peeled, cored, and sliced
- 1/4 cup unsalted butter
- 1/2 cup brown sugar
- 1 teaspoon ground cinnamon
- Pinch of salt

For the cake batter:

- 1 1/2 cups all-purpose flour
- 1 teaspoon baking powder
- 1/4 teaspoon baking soda
- 1/4 teaspoon salt
- 1/2 cup unsalted butter, softened
- 3/4 cup granulated sugar
- 2 large eggs
- 1 teaspoon vanilla extract
- 1/2 cup sour cream or Greek yogurt

Instructions:

1. Preheat your Dutch oven by placing coals beneath and on top of it. If you're using an oven, preheat it to 350°F (175°C).
2. In the Dutch oven, melt the 1/4 cup of unsalted butter over medium heat. Add the brown sugar, ground cinnamon, and pinch of salt, stirring until the sugar is dissolved and the mixture is bubbling.
3. Arrange the sliced pears in a single layer over the melted butter and sugar mixture in the Dutch oven. Cook for about 5-7 minutes, until the pears are slightly softened and caramelized. Remove from heat and set aside.
4. In a medium mixing bowl, whisk together the all-purpose flour, baking powder, baking soda, and salt. Set aside.

5. In a separate large mixing bowl, cream together the softened unsalted butter and granulated sugar until light and fluffy.
6. Beat in the eggs, one at a time, until well incorporated. Stir in the vanilla extract.
7. Gradually add the dry ingredients to the wet ingredients, alternating with the sour cream or Greek yogurt, and mixing until just combined.
8. Carefully spread the cake batter over the caramelized pear topping in the Dutch oven, smoothing it out evenly.
9. Cover the Dutch oven with its lid and place it over the preheated coals. If using an oven, place the Dutch oven on a baking sheet and bake for about 30-35 minutes, or until a toothpick inserted into the center of the cake comes out clean.
10. Once done, remove the Dutch oven from the heat or oven and let the upside-down pear cake cool slightly.
11. To serve, carefully invert the cake onto a serving platter, so the caramelized pear topping is on top.
12. Slice and serve the Dutch Oven Upside-Down Pear Cake warm or at room temperature. Enjoy the sweet and fruity flavors of this delightful dessert!

Dutch Oven Walnut Brownies

Ingredients:

- 1 cup unsalted butter
- 2 cups granulated sugar
- 4 large eggs
- 2 teaspoons vanilla extract
- 1 cup all-purpose flour
- 3/4 cup cocoa powder
- 1/4 teaspoon salt
- 1 cup chopped walnuts

Instructions:

1. Preheat your Dutch oven by placing coals beneath and on top of it. If you're using an oven, preheat it to 350°F (175°C).
2. Grease the bottom and sides of your Dutch oven with butter or cooking spray.
3. In a saucepan or microwave-safe bowl, melt the unsalted butter over low heat or in the microwave.
4. In a large mixing bowl, combine the melted butter and granulated sugar. Mix well.
5. Beat in the eggs, one at a time, until well combined.
6. Stir in the vanilla extract.
7. In a separate mixing bowl, sift together the all-purpose flour, cocoa powder, and salt.
8. Gradually add the dry ingredients to the wet ingredients, mixing until just combined.
9. Fold in the chopped walnuts until evenly distributed throughout the brownie batter.
10. Pour the brownie batter into the greased Dutch oven, spreading it out evenly.
11. Cover the Dutch oven with its lid and place it over the preheated coals. If using an oven, place the Dutch oven on a baking sheet and bake for about 25-30 minutes, or until a toothpick inserted into the center of the brownies comes out with a few moist crumbs.
12. Once done, remove the Dutch oven from the heat or oven and let the walnut brownies cool slightly.
13. Cut into squares and serve warm or at room temperature.

14. Enjoy the Dutch Oven Walnut Brownies with a glass of milk or your favorite hot beverage!

Dutch Oven Zucchini Bread

Ingredients:

- 1 1/2 cups shredded zucchini (about 1 medium zucchini)
- 1 cup granulated sugar
- 1/2 cup vegetable oil
- 2 large eggs
- 1 teaspoon vanilla extract
- 1 1/2 cups all-purpose flour
- 1/2 teaspoon baking powder
- 1/2 teaspoon baking soda
- 1/2 teaspoon salt
- 1 teaspoon ground cinnamon
- 1/4 teaspoon ground nutmeg
- 1/2 cup chopped walnuts or pecans (optional)

Instructions:

1. Preheat your Dutch oven by placing coals beneath and on top of it. If you're using an oven, preheat it to 350°F (175°C).
2. Grease the bottom and sides of your Dutch oven with butter or cooking spray.
3. In a large mixing bowl, combine the shredded zucchini, granulated sugar, vegetable oil, eggs, and vanilla extract. Mix until well combined.
4. In a separate mixing bowl, sift together the all-purpose flour, baking powder, baking soda, salt, ground cinnamon, and ground nutmeg.
5. Gradually add the dry ingredients to the wet ingredients, stirring until just combined. Do not overmix.
6. If desired, fold in the chopped walnuts or pecans until evenly distributed throughout the batter.
7. Pour the batter into the greased Dutch oven, spreading it out evenly.
8. Cover the Dutch oven with its lid and place it over the preheated coals. If using an oven, place the Dutch oven on a baking sheet and bake for about 50-60 minutes, or until a toothpick inserted into the center of the bread comes out clean.
9. Once done, remove the Dutch oven from the heat or oven and let the zucchini bread cool slightly.
10. Slice and serve the Dutch Oven Zucchini Bread warm or at room temperature.

11. Enjoy the moist and flavorful goodness of this classic quick bread!

Dutch Oven Cranberry Orange Cake

Ingredients:

For the cake:

- 1 cup granulated sugar
- 1/2 cup unsalted butter, softened
- 2 large eggs
- 1 teaspoon vanilla extract
- Zest of 1 orange
- 2 cups all-purpose flour
- 1 1/2 teaspoons baking powder
- 1/2 teaspoon baking soda
- 1/4 teaspoon salt
- 1 cup sour cream
- 1 cup fresh or frozen cranberries

For the glaze:

- 1 cup powdered sugar
- 2-3 tablespoons freshly squeezed orange juice
- Zest of 1 orange (optional)

Instructions:

1. Preheat your Dutch oven by placing coals beneath and on top of it. If you're using an oven, preheat it to 350°F (175°C).
2. Grease the bottom and sides of your Dutch oven with butter or cooking spray.
3. In a large mixing bowl, cream together the granulated sugar and softened unsalted butter until light and fluffy.
4. Beat in the eggs, one at a time, until well combined. Stir in the vanilla extract and orange zest.
5. In a separate mixing bowl, sift together the all-purpose flour, baking powder, baking soda, and salt.
6. Gradually add the dry ingredients to the wet ingredients, alternating with the sour cream, and mixing until just combined.
7. Gently fold in the cranberries until evenly distributed throughout the cake batter.

8. Pour the batter into the greased Dutch oven, spreading it out evenly.
9. Cover the Dutch oven with its lid and place it over the preheated coals. If using an oven, place the Dutch oven on a baking sheet and bake for about 40-45 minutes, or until a toothpick inserted into the center of the cake comes out clean.
10. Once done, remove the Dutch oven from the heat or oven and let the cranberry orange cake cool slightly.
11. While the cake is cooling, prepare the glaze. In a small bowl, whisk together the powdered sugar and freshly squeezed orange juice until smooth. Stir in the orange zest if desired.
12. Drizzle the glaze over the warm cake in the Dutch oven.
13. Let the cake cool completely before slicing and serving.
14. Serve the Dutch Oven Cranberry Orange Cake at room temperature. Enjoy the tangy and citrusy flavors of this delightful dessert!

Dutch Oven Maple Pecan Pie

Ingredients:

For the crust:

- 1 1/4 cups all-purpose flour
- 1/2 teaspoon salt
- 1/2 cup unsalted butter, chilled and diced
- 1/4 cup ice water

For the filling:

- 1 cup maple syrup
- 3/4 cup packed brown sugar
- 1/4 cup unsalted butter, melted
- 3 large eggs
- 1 teaspoon vanilla extract
- 1/4 teaspoon salt
- 2 cups pecan halves

Instructions:

1. Preheat your Dutch oven by placing coals beneath and on top of it. If you're using an oven, preheat it to 350°F (175°C).
2. To make the crust, in a large mixing bowl, combine the all-purpose flour and salt. Cut in the chilled and diced unsalted butter using a pastry cutter or your fingers until the mixture resembles coarse crumbs.
3. Gradually add the ice water to the flour mixture, a tablespoon at a time, mixing with a fork until the dough comes together. Shape the dough into a ball, flatten it into a disk, wrap it in plastic wrap, and refrigerate for at least 30 minutes.
4. Roll out the chilled dough on a lightly floured surface into a circle large enough to fit into the bottom and up the sides of the greased Dutch oven.
5. Press the rolled-out dough into the bottom and up the sides of the greased Dutch oven to form the crust.

6. In a large mixing bowl, whisk together the maple syrup, packed brown sugar, melted unsalted butter, eggs, vanilla extract, and salt until well combined.
7. Stir in the pecan halves until evenly coated in the maple syrup mixture.
8. Pour the pecan filling into the prepared crust in the Dutch oven, spreading it out evenly.
9. Cover the Dutch oven with its lid and place it over the preheated coals. If using an oven, place the Dutch oven on a baking sheet and bake for about 40-45 minutes, or until the filling is set and the crust is golden brown.
10. Once done, remove the Dutch oven from the heat or oven and let the maple pecan pie cool slightly.
11. Slice and serve the Dutch Oven Maple Pecan Pie warm or at room temperature.
12. Enjoy the sweet and nutty flavors of this delicious dessert!

Dutch Oven Apple Cranberry Crisp

Ingredients:

For the filling:

- 4-5 large apples, peeled, cored, and thinly sliced
- 1 cup fresh or frozen cranberries
- 1/4 cup granulated sugar
- 2 tablespoons all-purpose flour
- 1 teaspoon ground cinnamon
- 1/4 teaspoon ground nutmeg
- 1 tablespoon lemon juice

For the topping:

- 1 cup old-fashioned rolled oats
- 1/2 cup all-purpose flour
- 1/2 cup packed brown sugar
- 1/4 teaspoon ground cinnamon
- Pinch of salt
- 1/2 cup unsalted butter, melted

Instructions:

1. Preheat your Dutch oven by placing coals beneath and on top of it. If you're using an oven, preheat it to 375°F (190°C).
2. In a large mixing bowl, combine the sliced apples, cranberries, granulated sugar, all-purpose flour, ground cinnamon, ground nutmeg, and lemon juice. Toss until the fruit is evenly coated with the sugar and spices.
3. In another mixing bowl, prepare the topping by combining the rolled oats, all-purpose flour, packed brown sugar, ground cinnamon, and pinch of salt. Stir until well mixed.
4. Pour the melted unsalted butter over the oat mixture and mix until the butter is evenly incorporated and the mixture resembles coarse crumbs.
5. Spread the apple-cranberry mixture evenly in the bottom of the greased Dutch oven.
6. Sprinkle the oat topping over the fruit mixture, covering it completely.

7. Cover the Dutch oven with its lid and place it over the preheated coals. If using an oven, place the Dutch oven on a baking sheet and bake for about 35-40 minutes, or until the filling is bubbly and the topping is golden brown.
8. Once done, remove the Dutch oven from the heat or oven and let the apple cranberry crisp cool slightly.
9. Serve the Dutch Oven Apple Cranberry Crisp warm or at room temperature.
10. Enjoy the sweet-tart combination of apples and cranberries with the crispy oat topping!

Dutch Oven Chocolate Chip Cookie Bars

Ingredients:

- 1 cup (2 sticks) unsalted butter, melted
- 1 cup packed brown sugar
- 1/2 cup granulated sugar
- 2 large eggs
- 1 tablespoon vanilla extract
- 2 1/4 cups all-purpose flour
- 1 teaspoon baking soda
- 1/2 teaspoon salt
- 2 cups semisweet chocolate chips

Instructions:

1. Preheat your Dutch oven by placing coals beneath and on top of it. If you're using an oven, preheat it to 350°F (175°C).
2. Grease the bottom and sides of your Dutch oven with butter or cooking spray.
3. In a large mixing bowl, whisk together the melted unsalted butter, packed brown sugar, and granulated sugar until well combined.
4. Beat in the eggs, one at a time, until incorporated. Stir in the vanilla extract.
5. In a separate mixing bowl, sift together the all-purpose flour, baking soda, and salt.
6. Gradually add the dry ingredients to the wet ingredients, mixing until just combined.
7. Fold in the semisweet chocolate chips until evenly distributed throughout the cookie dough.
8. Press the cookie dough evenly into the greased Dutch oven.
9. Cover the Dutch oven with its lid and place it over the preheated coals. If using an oven, place the Dutch oven on a baking sheet and bake for about 25-30 minutes, or until the cookie bars are golden brown and set in the center.
10. Once done, remove the Dutch oven from the heat or oven and let the chocolate chip cookie bars cool slightly.
11. Cut into squares or bars and serve warm or at room temperature.
12. Enjoy the deliciousness of these Dutch Oven Chocolate Chip Cookie Bars with a glass of milk or your favorite hot beverage!

Dutch Oven Lemon Meringue Pie

Ingredients:

For the crust:

- 1 1/4 cups all-purpose flour
- 1/2 teaspoon salt
- 1/2 cup unsalted butter, chilled and diced
- 1/4 cup ice water

For the lemon filling:

- 1 cup granulated sugar
- 1/4 cup cornstarch
- 1/4 teaspoon salt
- 1 1/2 cups water
- 3 large egg yolks
- 1 tablespoon lemon zest
- 1/2 cup fresh lemon juice
- 2 tablespoons unsalted butter

For the meringue:

- 3 large egg whites
- 1/4 teaspoon cream of tartar
- 1/4 cup granulated sugar
- 1/2 teaspoon vanilla extract

Instructions:

1. Preheat your Dutch oven by placing coals beneath and on top of it. If you're using an oven, preheat it to 375°F (190°C).
2. To make the crust, in a large mixing bowl, combine the all-purpose flour and salt. Cut in the chilled and diced unsalted butter using a pastry cutter or your fingers until the mixture resembles coarse crumbs. Gradually add the ice water, a tablespoon at a time, mixing until the dough comes together. Shape the dough

into a ball, flatten it into a disk, wrap it in plastic wrap, and refrigerate for at least 30 minutes.
3. Roll out the chilled dough on a lightly floured surface into a circle large enough to fit into the bottom and up the sides of the greased Dutch oven. Press the rolled-out dough into the bottom and up the sides of the greased Dutch oven to form the crust.
4. Prick the bottom of the crust with a fork to prevent air bubbles from forming during baking. Bake the crust in the preheated Dutch oven for about 15-20 minutes, or until lightly golden brown. Remove from the oven and let cool slightly.
5. To make the lemon filling, in a saucepan, whisk together the granulated sugar, cornstarch, and salt. Gradually whisk in the water until smooth. Cook over medium heat, stirring constantly, until the mixture thickens and comes to a boil. Boil for 1 minute, then remove from heat.
6. In a separate mixing bowl, whisk the egg yolks until slightly thickened. Gradually whisk in about 1/2 cup of the hot sugar mixture to temper the yolks, then pour the egg mixture back into the saucepan with the remaining sugar mixture, whisking constantly. Cook over medium heat, stirring constantly, until the mixture thickens, about 2-3 minutes.
7. Remove the lemon filling from heat and stir in the lemon zest, lemon juice, and unsalted butter until smooth. Pour the lemon filling into the baked crust.
8. To make the meringue, in a clean mixing bowl, beat the egg whites and cream of tartar with an electric mixer on medium speed until soft peaks form. Gradually add the granulated sugar, 1 tablespoon at a time, beating on high speed until stiff peaks form. Beat in the vanilla extract.
9. Spoon the meringue over the hot lemon filling, spreading it to the edges of the crust to seal it completely.
10. Bake the pie in the preheated Dutch oven for about 10-15 minutes, or until the meringue is lightly golden brown.
11. Remove the Dutch oven from heat or oven and let the pie cool completely before serving.
12. Slice and serve the Dutch Oven Lemon Meringue Pie at room temperature. Enjoy the tangy lemon filling and fluffy meringue topping!

Dutch Oven Red Velvet Cake

Ingredients:

For the cake:

- 2 1/2 cups all-purpose flour
- 1 1/2 cups granulated sugar
- 1 teaspoon baking soda
- 1 teaspoon salt
- 1 teaspoon cocoa powder
- 1 1/2 cups vegetable oil
- 1 cup buttermilk, room temperature
- 2 large eggs, room temperature
- 2 tablespoons red food coloring
- 1 teaspoon vanilla extract
- 1 teaspoon white vinegar

For the cream cheese frosting:

- 8 ounces cream cheese, softened
- 1/2 cup unsalted butter, softened
- 4 cups powdered sugar
- 1 teaspoon vanilla extract

Instructions:

1. Preheat your Dutch oven by placing coals beneath and on top of it. If you're using an oven, preheat it to 350°F (175°C).
2. Grease the bottom and sides of your Dutch oven with butter or cooking spray.
3. In a large mixing bowl, sift together the all-purpose flour, granulated sugar, baking soda, salt, and cocoa powder.
4. In a separate mixing bowl, whisk together the vegetable oil, buttermilk, eggs, red food coloring, vanilla extract, and white vinegar until well combined.
5. Gradually add the wet ingredients to the dry ingredients, mixing until smooth and well combined.

6. Pour the batter into the greased Dutch oven, spreading it out evenly.
7. Cover the Dutch oven with its lid and place it over the preheated coals. If using an oven, place the Dutch oven on a baking sheet and bake for about 30-35 minutes, or until a toothpick inserted into the center of the cake comes out clean.
8. Once done, remove the Dutch oven from the heat or oven and let the red velvet cake cool slightly.
9. While the cake is cooling, prepare the cream cheese frosting. In a mixing bowl, beat together the softened cream cheese and unsalted butter until smooth and creamy. Gradually add the powdered sugar, one cup at a time, beating until smooth. Stir in the vanilla extract.
10. Spread the cream cheese frosting over the cooled red velvet cake in the Dutch oven.
11. Slice and serve the Dutch Oven Red Velvet Cake at room temperature.
12. Enjoy the rich and moist cake with its creamy frosting!

Dutch Oven Carrot Cake

Ingredients:

For the cake:

- 2 cups all-purpose flour
- 2 teaspoons baking powder
- 1 1/2 teaspoons baking soda
- 1/2 teaspoon salt
- 2 teaspoons ground cinnamon
- 1/2 teaspoon ground nutmeg
- 1/2 teaspoon ground ginger
- 1 1/2 cups granulated sugar
- 1 cup vegetable oil
- 4 large eggs
- 2 teaspoons vanilla extract
- 2 cups grated carrots
- 1 cup crushed pineapple, drained
- 1/2 cup shredded coconut (optional)
- 1/2 cup chopped walnuts or pecans (optional)
- 1/2 cup raisins (optional)

For the cream cheese frosting:

- 8 ounces cream cheese, softened
- 1/2 cup unsalted butter, softened
- 4 cups powdered sugar
- 1 teaspoon vanilla extract

Instructions:

1. Preheat your Dutch oven by placing coals beneath and on top of it. If you're using an oven, preheat it to 350°F (175°C).
2. Grease the bottom and sides of your Dutch oven with butter or cooking spray.

3. In a large mixing bowl, sift together the all-purpose flour, baking powder, baking soda, salt, ground cinnamon, ground nutmeg, and ground ginger.
4. In another mixing bowl, whisk together the granulated sugar, vegetable oil, eggs, and vanilla extract until well combined.
5. Gradually add the wet ingredients to the dry ingredients, mixing until just combined.
6. Fold in the grated carrots, crushed pineapple, shredded coconut (if using), chopped walnuts or pecans (if using), and raisins (if using) until evenly distributed throughout the batter.
7. Pour the batter into the greased Dutch oven, spreading it out evenly.
8. Cover the Dutch oven with its lid and place it over the preheated coals. If using an oven, place the Dutch oven on a baking sheet and bake for about 40-45 minutes, or until a toothpick inserted into the center of the cake comes out clean.
9. Once done, remove the Dutch oven from the heat or oven and let the carrot cake cool slightly.
10. While the cake is cooling, prepare the cream cheese frosting. In a mixing bowl, beat together the softened cream cheese and unsalted butter until smooth and creamy. Gradually add the powdered sugar, one cup at a time, beating until smooth. Stir in the vanilla extract.
11. Spread the cream cheese frosting over the cooled carrot cake in the Dutch oven.
12. Slice and serve the Dutch Oven Carrot Cake at room temperature.
13. Enjoy the moist and flavorful cake with its creamy frosting!

Dutch Oven Mint Chocolate Chip Brownies

Ingredients:

- 1/2 cup (1 stick) unsalted butter
- 1 cup granulated sugar
- 2 large eggs
- 1 teaspoon vanilla extract
- 1/2 cup all-purpose flour
- 1/3 cup unsweetened cocoa powder
- 1/4 teaspoon salt
- 1/4 teaspoon baking powder
- 1/2 cup mint chocolate chips

Instructions:

1. Preheat your Dutch oven by placing coals beneath and on top of it. If you're using an oven, preheat it to 350°F (175°C).
2. Grease the bottom and sides of your Dutch oven with butter or cooking spray.
3. In a saucepan or microwave-safe bowl, melt the unsalted butter over low heat or in the microwave.
4. In a large mixing bowl, combine the melted butter and granulated sugar. Mix well.
5. Beat in the eggs, one at a time, until well combined. Stir in the vanilla extract.
6. In a separate mixing bowl, sift together the all-purpose flour, cocoa powder, salt, and baking powder.
7. Gradually add the dry ingredients to the wet ingredients, mixing until just combined.
8. Fold in the mint chocolate chips until evenly distributed throughout the brownie batter.
9. Pour the batter into the greased Dutch oven, spreading it out evenly.
10. Cover the Dutch oven with its lid and place it over the preheated coals. If using an oven, place the Dutch oven on a baking sheet and bake for about 20-25 minutes, or until a toothpick inserted into the center of the brownies comes out with a few moist crumbs.
11. Once done, remove the Dutch oven from the heat or oven and let the mint chocolate chip brownies cool slightly.
12. Cut into squares and serve warm or at room temperature.

13. Enjoy the Dutch Oven Mint Chocolate Chip Brownies with a glass of milk or your favorite hot beverage!

Dutch Oven Coconut Cream Pie

Ingredients:

For the crust:

- 1 1/2 cups graham cracker crumbs
- 1/4 cup granulated sugar
- 1/3 cup unsalted butter, melted

For the filling:

- 1 cup granulated sugar
- 1/4 cup cornstarch
- 1/2 teaspoon salt
- 3 cups whole milk
- 4 large egg yolks
- 1 cup sweetened shredded coconut
- 2 teaspoons vanilla extract
- 2 tablespoons unsalted butter

For the topping:

- 1 cup heavy cream
- 2 tablespoons powdered sugar
- 1/2 cup sweetened shredded coconut, toasted (optional)

Instructions:

1. Preheat your Dutch oven by placing coals beneath and on top of it. If you're using an oven, preheat it to 350°F (175°C).
2. To make the crust, in a mixing bowl, combine the graham cracker crumbs, granulated sugar, and melted unsalted butter. Press the mixture into the bottom and up the sides of a greased Dutch oven to form the crust.

3. Bake the crust in the preheated Dutch oven for about 8-10 minutes, or until lightly golden brown. Remove from the oven and let it cool slightly.
4. To make the filling, in a saucepan, whisk together the granulated sugar, cornstarch, and salt. Gradually whisk in the whole milk until smooth. Cook over medium heat, stirring constantly, until the mixture thickens and comes to a boil.
5. In a separate mixing bowl, whisk the egg yolks until slightly thickened. Gradually whisk in about 1/2 cup of the hot milk mixture to temper the yolks, then pour the egg mixture back into the saucepan with the remaining milk mixture, whisking constantly. Cook over medium heat, stirring constantly, until the mixture thickens, about 2-3 minutes.
6. Remove the filling from heat and stir in the sweetened shredded coconut, vanilla extract, and unsalted butter until smooth. Pour the filling into the cooled crust in the Dutch oven, spreading it out evenly.
7. To make the topping, in a mixing bowl, beat the heavy cream and powdered sugar until stiff peaks form. Spread the whipped cream over the coconut filling in the Dutch oven.
8. If desired, sprinkle the toasted sweetened shredded coconut over the whipped cream topping.
9. Cover the Dutch oven with its lid and place it in the refrigerator for at least 4 hours, or until the pie is chilled and set.
10. Once chilled, slice and serve the Dutch Oven Coconut Cream Pie.
11. Enjoy the creamy coconut filling and fluffy whipped cream topping in this delightful dessert!